Foreword

It is a great privilege to be asked to write the foreword to a book entitled 'The Most Famous Book in The World' because the Bible is simply that. Over the centuries it has been a source of inspiration, comfort, challenge, wisdom and truth as well as theological study for millions and is still the best selling book across the globe.

Ultimately, it speaks truth because it is the Word of God. For Christians across the globe it is His divine revelation of Himself, and if we lose that, we lose our identity in Christ. It is a voice to be listened to in our daily lives. And it has shaped our culture over centuries.

It is, quite simply, an amazing book! When asked which he would prefer children to be taught in schools, the former Poet Laureate, Sir Andrew Motion chose the Bible over Shakespeare. Professor Richard Dawkins, the well known atheist, also recently said:

"You can't appreciate English literature unless you are steeped to some extent in the King James Bible. People don't know that proverbial phrases which make echoes in their minds come from this Bible. We are a Christian culture, we come from a Christian culture and not to know the King James Bible, is to be in some small way, barbarian."

In short it is in our cultural DNA.

The history of the Jewish nation, the beauty and the poetry of the Psalms and the teachings of Jesus Christ make the Bible a source of inspiration for each of us – be we Christian, Agnostic or Atheist; though the contributors to this book are all Christians.

The book is an easy read, designed to be dipped into or given as a present, a complement to other books produced to mark the 400th anniversary of the King James Bible. My hope is that those people who don't read Scripture may be intrigued and inspired by the contributors list and start reading the Bible themselves.

Today the Bible is available in audio and Braille, on smart phones and the web. In 400 years since the King James Bible was translated, the format may have changed but God's words and His message to us do not. They remain the greatest love letter humankind has ever received.

Canon Dr Ann Holt OBE
Director of Programme, British and Foreign Bible Society

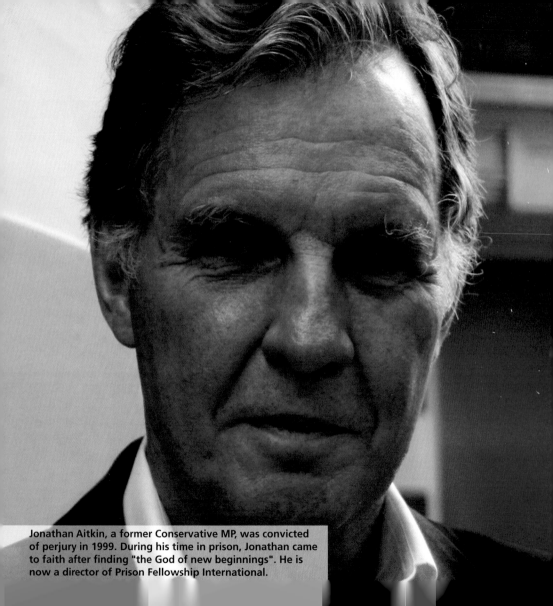

Jonathan Aitkin, a former Conservative MP, was convicted of perjury in 1999. During his time in prison, Jonathan came to faith after finding "the God of new beginnings". He is now a director of Prison Fellowship International.

Jonathan Aitken

Psalm 130 v 1-2

> 1 Out of the depths have I cried unto thee, O LORD.
> 2 Lord, hear my voice: let thine ears be attentive to the voice of my supplications.
>
> Psalm 130 v 1-2

These opening words of one of the Bible's great penitential psalms have resonated down the millennia to people in trouble. This is because most of us sink into the depths at some stage of our lives. Illness, bereavement, broken relationships, depression, imprisonment, exile, or heartbreak in its many forms are just some all too familiar 'in the depths' experiences. What they have in common is that they usually cannot be overcome by our own will power. Climbing out of the depths needs the help of God's power.

The use of the word 'cry' sometimes means tears but it always means prayers. The secular expression, 'if you're in a hole stop digging', should be amended in the light of this psalm to, 'if you're in a hole start praying.'

Augustine of Hippo, who loved Psalm 130, commented on its opening verses saying, 'When we cry to our Lord from the depths he heareth our cry and the very cry itself suffereth us to move from the bottom.' In modern language it might be said that prayer is the starter motor of the soul's climb out of the depths.

I discovered this psalm in a prison cell when I was in the depths of the very public agonies of defeat, disgrace, divorce, bankruptcy and jail. The beautiful cadences of the King James Version spoke to me. I have read, re-read and prayed Psalm 130 innumerable times, finding its spiritual message a true lantern to my feet, signposting God's path out of life's depths.

Steve Chalke founded the Oasis Trust. Oasis now has just under 2000 staff, and pioneers educational, healthcare and housing initiatives in the UK and across the globe.

Steve Chalke

Genesis 1 v 27

> 27 So God created man in his own image, in the image of God created he him; male and female created he them.
> Genesis 1 v 27

A friend of mine – Stephen Ferguson said, "I am a barrister, I defend criminals. My clients are terrorists, murderers, armed robbers, international drug traffickers, city fraudsters, money launderers and the heads of a couple of well known criminal families. But ask me, can I see the image of God in them? My heartfelt answer is resoundingly in the affirmative."

He is not alone. In the 4th Century St. Augustine taught, 'Although worn out and defaced… yet the image of God still remains.' Each and every one of us, however far we have wandered from God, continues to bear His imprint.

Amongst the nations that surrounded ancient Israel, only the king was regarded as being made in the image of the local deity. So, it is into this world laden with oppressive hierarchy, dictatorship and sexism, which viewed ordinary people as nothing more than the pawns of the powerful, that God speaks. Genesis 1 v 27 declares that every man and every woman bears God's image – that the whole of humankind enjoys this irreversible privilege and responsibility, one that even though scarred and maimed by our rebellion and self-centredness, remains indelible.

We are still on the first page of the Bible and the revolution of the God of love has already begun!

Genesis 1 v 27 has had, and continues to have, a more profound and challenging impact on me than perhaps any other. For instance, I remember that when Oasis first began working with homeless men, many of whom were alcoholics, I slowly learned to look into their eyes and recognise the image of God; it transformed the way I treated them. As I have learned to see the reflection of God in the face of those I work with day-by-day, however awkward their opinions might be to me, it has slowly pushed me to re-evaluate my approach and attitudes to the views of others. In short, it has reshaped my life, teaching me to value diversity rather than to despise it.

The founder and CEO of the Humanitarian Aid Relief Trust, Baroness Cox was created a life peer in 1982 and was Deputy Speaker of House of Lords from 1985 to 2005.

Baroness Caroline Cox

Joshua 1 v 9

> 9 Have not I commanded thee? Be strong and of a good courage; be not afraid, neither be thou dismayed: for the LORD thy God *is* with thee whithersoever thou goest.
>
> Joshua 1 v 9

This was the text given by the Bishop at my confirmation and it has meant a great deal to me over the many years since!

I have to confess in the course of my work I am often afraid and dismayed. I am, however, privileged to spend considerable time with people suffering from oppression and persecution in some of the darkest parts of the world as I believe it is important to spend time with them - to show solidarity, to try to offer aid according to their needs and to underpin advocacy, when I try to tell their stories.

Sometimes this means I must travel to places of conflict; always it means being with people who are suffering in some way from 'man's inhumanity to man'. I am afraid and dismayed before leaving for these visits, as I know they will be challenging in many ways: personally, as my faith seems so small and pathetic compared to theirs; and sometimes physically, living, albeit only for a short time, in conditions rather different from the security and comforts we tend to take for granted in our own 'comfort zones'.

But when I do feel afraid and dismayed I remember two things: firstly, that God's words were a 'command' - not just an invitation! Secondly, I know that when I do have the privilege of being with brothers and sisters suffering on the front lines of faith and freedom, I will be so blessed by their faith, courage, dignity and miracles of grace, that I will return, receiving more than I can ever give.

But I do still need to remind myself of this, my confirmation text!

3 Blessed are the poor in spirit: for theirs is the kingdom of heaven.

4 Blessed are they that mourn: for they shall be comforted.

5 Blessed are the meek: for they shall inherit the earth.

6 Blessed are they which do hunger and thirst after righteousness: for they shall be filled.

7 Blessed are the merciful: for they shall obtain mercy.

8 Blessed are the pure in heart: for they shall see God.

9 Blessed are the peace-makers: for they shall be called the children of God.

10 Blessed are they which are persecuted for righteousness' sake: for theirs is the kingdom of heaven.

11 Blessed are ye, when men shall revile you, and persecute you, and shall say all manner of evil against you falsely, for my sake.

12 Rejoice, and be exceeding glad: for great is your reward in heaven: for so persecuted they the prophets which were before you.

Matthew 5 v 3-12

Sir Tom Farmer founded the Kwik-Fit empire and was awarded the Andrew Carnegie Medal of Philanthropy in 2005.

Sir Tom Farmer

Matthew 5 v 3-12

I am the youngest of seven children and was brought up in a strong Catholic household in Leith near Edinburgh. Ours was a busy but loving house. As a child I used to think my mother never slept because she was awake when I went to bed and awake when I got up. With seven children to look after, there was always something to do.

My parents had a strong faith and passed it on to us. We were at church every Sunday and the parish was the centre of our lives; it provided spiritual nourishment and great dances on a Saturday night. I met my wife Anne at a parish dance. She has been the best wife, mother and business advisor.

Our religious education started in the home. As children, my parents taught us it was important to always respect God and respect our fellow man. Often my mother, when trying to sort out the squabbles amongst her children would quote Jesus from the Beatitudes saying, 'Blessed are the Peace Makers.'

I regularly reflect on the Beatitudes today. They apply to every aspect of our lives, including business. I don't agree with people who say there's no room in business for Christian principles. Good successful businesses have high moral standards that are based on the principles of the Beatitudes.

When you have a business where people are treated with respect and paid a fair wage, when you pay your suppliers on time and honour contracts, you can enjoy your wealth and share it with others. That's righteousness.

Nicky Gumbel, a former atheist, is now the public face of the worldwide Alpha course. Since 1993 more than 15 million people have completed the Alpha course in 163 countries around the world.

7 Beloved, let us love one another: for love is of God; and every one that loveth is born of God, and knoweth God.

8 He that loveth not knoweth not God; for God is love.

9 In this was manifested the love of God toward us, because that God sent his only begotten Son into the world, that we might live through him.

10 Herein is love, not that we loved God, but that he loved us, and sent his Son [to be] the propitiation for our sins.

11 Beloved, if God so loved us, we ought also to love one another.

12 No man hath seen God at any time. If we love one another, God dwelleth in us, and his love is perfected in us.

16 And we have known and believed the love that God hath to us. God is love; and he that dwelleth in love dwelleth in God, and God in him.

17 Herein is our love made perfect, that we may have boldness in the day of judgment: because as he is, so are we in this world.

18 There is no fear in love; but perfect love casteth out fear: because fear hath torment. He that feareth is not made perfect in love.

19 We love him, because he first loved us.

20 If a man say, I love God, and hateth his brother, he is a liar: for he that loveth not his brother whom he hath seen, how can he love God whom he hath not seen?

21 And this commandment have we from him, That he who loveth God love his brother also.

1 John 4 v 7–12 & 16–21

If I were asked to summarise what I thought the Bible was all about in one word – apart from the word 'Jesus' – I would choose the word 'love'. Twice in this passage John writes, 'God is love'. The word 'love' is used very widely in our society. Nowhere in the Bible does it say 'Love is God'. In other words, it is God who defines what love means rather than the other way round.

This passage can be summed up very simply. Firstly, it all starts with God's love for us. How do we know God loves us? We know because He showed His love by sending Jesus in to the world to die for us so that we might have life. 'Herein is love, not that we loved God, but that he loved us, and sent his Son to be the propitiation for our sins'.

Secondly, our love for God – our response to God's love to us is to love Him. 'We love him because he first loved us.' In this love relationship with God we are given confidence on the day of judgement. 'There is no fear in love; but perfect love casteth out fear: because fear hath torment. He that feareth is not made perfect in love' (v 18).

This is how it is intended that we should live – in a perfect love relationship with God, knowing and experiencing His love for us and responding in fearless love.

And finally, our love for one another - out of this love relationship with God flows love for others. It is the evidence that we have experienced His love and that we love Him. 'Beloved, if God so loved us, we ought also to love one another. No man hath seen God at any time. If we love one another, God dwelleth in us, and his love is perfected in us.'

Sir John Houghton was co-chairman of the Scientific Assessment Group of the Intergovernmental Panel on Climate Change. He is also the Chairman of the John Ray Initiative, an organisation connecting environment, science and Christianity.

Professor John Houghton

Proverbs 8 v 30-31

> 30 Then I was by him, *as* one brought up *with him:* and I was daily *his* delight, rejoicing always before him;
> 31 Rejoicing in the habitable part of his earth; and my delights *were* with the sons of men.
>
> Proverbs 8 v 30-31

I am a scientist and feel very privileged to have spent my life studying creation with all its fascination and wonder. In this eloquent passage in Proverbs that begins at verse 22, wisdom is speaking of working with God in creation, the craftsman at His side, rejoicing together in the whole process of creation. Because we are also creative, made in the image of God, we too can share in the sheer delight enjoyed by God the creator.

In the New Testament, this personified divine wisdom is identified with Jesus. In the early verses of John's Gospel, Jesus is described as the agent of creation, the one through whom all things were made. Paul describes Jesus as the creator and sustainer of the universe – the one by whom all things were created and as the one in whom all things hold together. It is in Jesus, the word made flesh that the spiritual and the material come together. The whole of creation is involved.

Some scientists today try to tell us that science has ruled out belief in God. But science only addresses the how of creation not the why. The laws of gravity, thermodynamics or quantum mechanics – and many more, we call them the laws of nature – are not invented by science. Rather scientists discover them. They originate with the creator.

Many of those who pioneered the development of modern science 300 or 400 years ago were Christians who talked of 'The Two Books' – God's revelations in His works and in His word. These are not to be viewed separately but together. As humans we have two eyes to view the world; their combined binocular vision brings depth not available to either eye on its own. As I have sought to put my science and faith alongside each other, the combination of my material eye and my spiritual eye has brought a richness beyond my imagination.

J John has been described as the funniest evangelist in the world, using humour, passion and theological insight, to help people discover spiritual meaning in their everyday lives.

Amen is a curious little word. It is used 159 times in the Bible. The word 'Amen' basically means 'be true'. It was a word that Jews used to confirm or agree with something, whether it was a prayer or a blessing. In modern English speech it means 'so be it', 'let it be so' or even 'let what we have said be binding on us'.

By using the word 'Amen' at the end of a prayer, a Jew of Jesus' day would have been making that prayer their own. Let me give you two illustrations of what 'Amen' means.

Firstly, 'Amen' is like the signature at the end of a contract. Until a contract is signed it is merely words and has no value. It is only binding when a signature is put at the end. By signing our name we are saying, "I agree with it and I allow myself to be bound by its terms." So when we say 'Amen' we are adding our verbal signature to what we have just prayed.

Secondly, 'Amen' is like raising your hand to vote for a motion. Imagine you are in a tense meeting of a small committee and a proposal is set out. Finally it comes to those crucial words, "All those in favour?" By raising your hand you are saying, "I vote for this – I am committed to it."

So saying 'Amen' at the end of a prayer or a biblical statement is a decisive act of commitment to or agreement with what has been prayed. It is not to be taken lightly.

There is, however, another aspect to 'Amen'. If 'Amen' is an expression of our commitment or agreement to God's purposes there is also in it a longing that God's purposes will be worked out. By saying 'Amen' we are asking God to bring what we have read in the Bible and prayed to fulfilment.

Next time you read the Bible or say a prayer, don't just say, 'Amen.' Pause and ask yourself some questions: Am I prepared to commit myself to what I have read and prayed? Am I prepared to live in a way that is consistent with my prayer? Am I prepared for God to answer my prayers?

If you are, then go ahead and say, 'Amen' to God's Word.

Described as the 'king of one-liners', Milton Jones is a multi-award winning comedian and a regular panellist on the BBC's Mock the Week and Michael McIntyre's Comedy Roadshow.

Milton Jones

Job 39 v 1

> 1 Knowest thou the time when the wild goats of the rock bring forth?
> Job 39 v 1

This is part of God's answer to Job – the world's 'unluckiest' man. He has a hundred, apparently reasonable and angry questions, and his friends aren't helping. Surely God has some explaining to do? This is one of God's answers, and it isn't an answer at all. Not specifically. He says other stuff about other animals and weather too, but, "Do you know when the mountain goat is born?" pretty much sums up God's response. What I get from it is:

"You know that animal that permanently lives a shaky hoof-step away from certain death. Yeah? Well, you know it's even more vulnerable offspring? Hmmm? Do you know when they arrive?"

"No?" (Never mind how they stay safe and well!)

There's no point in replying really. Point taken. Jesus often answered a question with another question. Not to avoid answering the question, but to answer the question in a more profound way.

To get to the real answer, of the real question. There are some things that can only be explained from where God is, outside time and space. To be angry is futile. What I need to do is trust.

I moan about the petty suffering and injustice in my life and occasionally some of the troubles in the rest of the world. But much of it is whining from my point of view – what I think God should be doing. It's not fair. His answer is gentle but profound. "I'm God – you're a man. What do you know?"

Fair enough.

Jeff Lucas lives in Colorado with wife, Kay, where he holds a teaching post at Timberline Church, Fort Collins. He is also an ambassador for Compassion, which helps children in poverty worldwide.

Jeff Lucas

> 7 Casting all your care upon him; for he careth for you.
>
> 1 Peter 5 v 7

I stared up at the words, written decades earlier in gothic script. 'He careth for you.' Sunday after Sunday, that would be the first message to greet me as I filed in. Some services were more engaging than others. On hot summer Sunday mornings, when the sun cascaded through stained glass windows, and dust danced in the distilled rays, and when the sermon seemed longer than usual, I would fix my eyes on that promise.

To know that there is a God is a cataclysmic discovery that changes everything. It's impossible to nod at His existence, to acknowledge His reality like a vaguely interested passer-by. But the greater truth is this – not only that there is a God, but what kind of person He is. Is He the stern, distant, cold Victorian papa? Worse still, is He the trembling-with-rage cosmic judge, His finger perilously close to the smite button?

He cares. And His care is not general, generic, vague. He cares for me. He knows my name, where I live. My greatest hopes, my secret nightmares, the best and worst of me – all of this is known. And that means that His love is no besotted romance that can be dashed and destroyed by reality. He won't wake up tomorrow and decide that His love for me is ended. He cares.

Commissioner Matear is Territorial President of Women's Ministries for the Salvation Army and Moderator of the Free Churches Group in England and Wales.

Commissioner Elizabeth Matear

Romans 15 v 13

> 13 Now the God of hope fill you with all joy and peace in believing, that ye may abound in hope, through the power of the Holy Ghost.
>
> Romans 15 v 13

My favourite phrase in this verse is 'the God of hope'. In these very short words there is both a cosmic dimension and a personal encounter. In a general sense 'hope' is often understood as optimism or positive thinking. Yet that is a limited and even erroneous understanding. Hope is a theological reality that comes from God.

As we understand who God is, all-powerful, all-gracious, everywhere present and the creator and governor of all things, then we know that our hope is way and above 'hoping against hope' or 'hoping for the best' or having 'high hopes'. The focus and centre of our hope is God from whom hope flows and with whom we must develop a relationship, so that we know Him.

The hope that we have means we need not be hopeless, nor manipulated by past failure. Hope is knowing that God will do what He says He will do. Therefore we can confidently endure situations where we might feel weary or drained. We can persevere when times are rough and heavy, 'Rejoicing in hope; patient in tribulation...' (Romans 12 v 13). Hope perseveres, sustains and encourages and looks forward to what will be.

As we build up our relationship with God, so we 'may abound in hope through the power of the Holy Ghost.' (Romans 15 v 13). We can be filled by hope.

We are motivated and compelled to share the God of hope with others. There are those who touch our lives who are without hope, who are helpless and even hostile as a result. We are directed to share the message of hope in the world, be it global or local. With hope in our hearts we work to share God's love throughout the world.

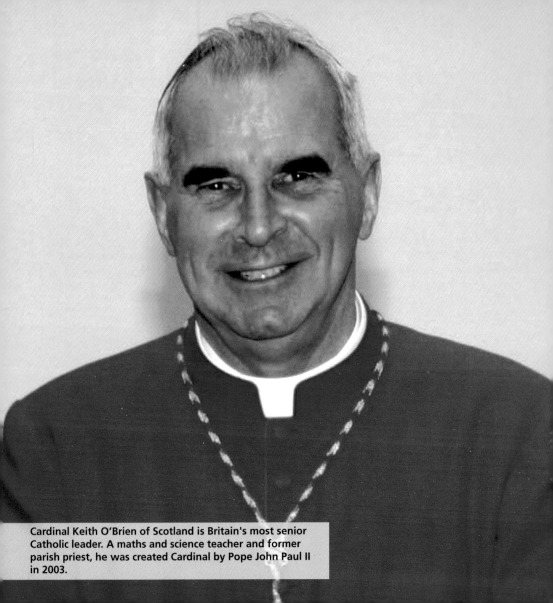

Cardinal Keith O'Brien of Scotland is Britain's most senior Catholic leader. A maths and science teacher and former parish priest, he was created Cardinal by Pope John Paul II in 2003.

Cardinal Keith O'Brien of Scotland

Mark 4 v 26-32

26 And he said, So is the kingdom of God, as if a man should cast seed into the ground;
27 And should sleep, and rise night and day, and the seed should spring and grow up, he knoweth not how.
28 For the earth bringeth forth fruit of herself; first the blade, then the ear, after that the full corn in the ear.
29 But when the fruit is brought forth, immediately he putteth in the sickle, because the harvest is come.
30 And he said, Whereunto shall we liken the kingdom of God? or with what comparison shall we compare it?
31 It is like a grain of mustard seed, which, when it is sown in the earth, is less than all the seeds that be in the earth:
32 But when it is sown, it groweth up, and becometh greater than all herbs, and shooteth out great branches; so that the fowls of the air may lodge under the shadow of it.

Mark 4 v 26-32

This passage particularly appeals to me because it shows that no matter our own human frailty or lack of knowledge or weariness in our mission, there is always some result for what we do. I specifically like the phrase regarding the sower, 'and the seed should spring and grow up, he knoweth not how.' It is a very beautiful parable and I find great encouragement in the verse, 'for the earth bringeth forth fruit of herself...'

I take particular consolation from this passage, both with regard to my apostolate within my own church diocese and my country of Scotland, as well as the apostolates in which I take part in various parts of the world; particularly those where the gospel is gradually and slowly growing, while in other countries the principles of the gospel are not being observed in any way.

I do not know just how the seed grows, but I do know that it does grow and that the harvest will be reaped in due time.

Peter Owen-Jones is an Anglican vicar with three rural parishes. Before being ordained, he worked as a farm labourer and ran a mobile disco.

Peter Owen-Jones

Psalm 23

1 The LORD *is* my shepherd; I shall not want.
2 He maketh me to lie down in green pastures: he leadeth me beside the still waters.
3 He restoreth my soul: he leadeth me in the paths of righteousness for his name's sake.
4 Yea, though I walk through the valley of the shadow of death, I will fear no evil: for thou *art* with me; thy rod and thy staff they comfort me.
5 Thou preparest a table before me in the presence of mine enemies: thou anointest my head with oil; my cup runneth over.
6 Surely goodness and mercy shall follow me all the days of my life: and I will dwell in the house of the LORD for ever.

Psalm 23

I cannot think of any other combination of words that invite us to consider the location of beauty in such a direct manner. King David is singing about our inner world; the still waters, the paths of righteousness.

The translation is unambiguously poetic and perhaps the reason why the King James version has survived and spoken for as long as it has is that it brings us to a point of innocence again and again. It is rooted in a pastoral world, connected to the land and the sea, the deserts and the woods.

Now we assume we have moved away from the natural thrill of the elemental but I am not sure that is possible and however urbanised we become there is still the truth of all life carrying one life and one life carrying all life and one all loving God filling our cup and anointing our head with oil.

Professor Sir Ghillean Prance was Director of the Royal Botanic Gardens, Kew. He is now Scientific Director at the Eden Project in Cornwall.

Professor Sir Ghillean Prance

Isaiah 41 v 19-20

> 19 I will plant in the wilderness the cedar, the shittah tree, and the myrtle, and the oil tree: I will set in the desert the fir tree, and the pine, and the box tree together:
> 20 That they may see, and know, and consider and understand together, that the hand of the Lord hath done this, and the Holy One of Israel hath created it.
>
> Isaiah 41 v 19-20

I have chosen these two verses because they not only reaffirm that the environment around us is the creation of God, but also indicate some of its purpose. God has revealed Himself in two ways: through the Bible and through the wonders of His creation.

In this passage our attention is drawn to some common trees of the Middle East; the majestic cedar, the acaia (shi-tah), the myrtle, the olive, the fir, the box and the pine. In these days of accelerated destruction of the environment, loss of biodiversity (including the trees listed in these verses) and climate change, it is good to return to the Bible and see what it says about creation. Here it is clearly stated that the wonders of creation and some of the splendid trees of the Bible lands are for us to see, know, consider, and understand that the hand of the Lord has created it.

This is one of the many scriptures that encourages me as a Christian and a conservationist to strive for the preservation of the environment because it is the creation of God.

The former Portsmouth FC defender, Linvoy Primus
launched Faith & Football with fellow player, Darren Moore.
Its aim is to support a range of community programmes
using football as a platform for relationship building.

Linvoy Primus

Jeremiah 29 v 11

> 11 For I know the thoughts that I think toward you, saith the LORD, thoughts of peace, and not of evil, to give you an expected end.
>
> Jeremiah 29 v 11

This verse came into my life at a time when I was struggling with my faith and trying to work out what God required of me in the ultra-competitive and macho world of professional football. I was finding it hard to gain acceptance as a new Christian with my football team-mates after I had 'gone public' with my conversion, and also trying to make sense of all the uncertainty surrounding my football career.

Out of the blue I received a letter from a young Portsmouth football fan that was so timely and gave me such a boost. He sent me this verse with a brief note saying, "I believe this scripture is for you." I was stunned by this verse which gave me such hope and, at the time, reinforced my strong belief that my life was really going to be taken care of.

I knew that God still needed my co-operation and that it was up to me to do everything to the best of my ability to ensure that His plan was fulfilled. From then on I felt I needed to be sensitive and obedient to what He was guiding me to do, otherwise I would end up making the wrong decisions and being in the wrong place. Those words from Jeremiah have been so important to me, and I suspect many others, and have resounded in my mind so often.

Dr John Sentamu was appointed as Archbishop of York in 2005. Born in rural Uganda, he fled to Britain in 1974 under persecution from Idi Amin.

> 10 The thief cometh not, but for to steal, and to kill, and to destroy: I am come that they might have life, and that they might have it more abundantly.
>
> John 10 v 10

What a contrast! Bad intentions versus the best of intentions. The next verse begins with one of our Lord's titles for Himself, 'The Good Shepherd'. In 1st Century Palestine, shepherds stayed night and day with their flocks. They led them, fed them and protected them from predators and rustlers, animal and human; would-be intruders and sheep-stealers were a constant threat.

Christ is the shepherd; we are the sheep. He watches over us night and day. So who are the marauders in this verse, who would mislead or abuse us, or abandon us when danger looms? History is littered with false prophets. They must have been plausible, persuasive and seemingly genuine. Some of their followers handed over all their money, joined exploitative communes, even committed mass suicide. Other false guides have taught that the human yearning for fulfilment can be satisfied by accumulating more and more possessions.

The best protection we have against our own gullibility is to put our trust in Christ and not be deviated from that. This biblical passage continues with an even more telling statement about the Good Shepherd's care, 'I lay down my life for the sheep.' Looking back, we know how that became a reality. He died for us. That is how much we matter to Him. God's sacrificial care for His creation has given a new meaning to the word 'love'.

As we receive God's love we also discover a new quality of life: 'abundant life' is how the Lord describes it. There's nothing cramped or constricting about it. Christians find themselves achieving things with God's help which would have been beyond their imagination without it. They have discovered that giving is more fun than getting; serving other people is more rewarding than being waited on; and a God-centred life is the reality for which we were created. That's abundant life!

Mandy Smith was just 18 when she married Rolling Stones' bass guitarist, Bill Wyman. She became one of the world's top models and enjoyed a successful singing career with Stock Aitkin Waterman.

Mandy Smith

Luke 15 v 20

> 20 And he arose, and came to his father. But when he was yet a great way off, his father saw him, and had compassion, and ran, and fell on his neck, and kissed him.
>
> Luke 15 v 20

When I returned to my faith, it was gradual. I'd be out shopping or on my way home from the office and come across a church that was open. I'd pop in and sit for maybe five minutes, maybe twenty. I'd say a prayer like, "Hey, Jesus, it's Mandy here." Other times, I'd read a Bible or just sit in silence. It was in the stillness of many different churches of different denominations, that I heard Jesus' comforting voice.

There are two lessons from my experience which I know are shared by many people. Firstly, praise God for churches that are left unlocked during the day. Church really is too good just for Sundays.

Secondly, many people say they feel God has left them. That is not so. It is we who leave Him. Like the father in Jesus' parable, God is always watching out for us. He runs to us and puts His arm around us and says, "Hey, good to see you."

No matter what we do or how far away we go, no matter what mess we get ourselves into, the Father is always there, looking out for us, filled with compassion. He longs for our return.

Martin Smith was a founder member of the Christian rock band Delirious? His best known songs include 'I could sing of your love forever' and 'History Maker'.

Martin Smith

Psalm 5 v 1-3

> 1 Give ear to my words, O LORD, consider my meditation.
> 2 Hearken unto the voice of my cry, my King, and my God: for unto thee will I pray.
> 3 My voice shalt thou hear in the morning, O LORD; in the morning will I direct *my prayer* unto thee, and will look up.
>
> Psalm 5 v 1-3

I love this psalm. During the last two years I have been drawn to this scripture time and time again. Having entered a new season and travelling through the pain of transition, this seems to sum up completely the plea of a human being crying out, firstly that God will not abandon him, and secondly that God will take his life as a sacrifice for the bigger cause. The more life goes on I realize that sacrifice is more important than success. We strive for so long to achieve our goals, obtain recognition and generally work our way up the ladder that we can forget what we were created for in the first place.

It's an amazing relief to know that we were born because He loves us, not because of what we can do for God. The notion that we are on this planet to help it along in some way is wide of the mark. Of course we bring our life and humanity to 'colour' the world, but God does not need you and me to save the universe. He simply wants us to love Him.

It's an incredible thought to ponder that we were simply created to love God, to worship Him, to adore Him, be His friend. Anything else is background noise and yet we long to find affirmation in worldly things. It's no surprise then that we can live a hollow existence looking for joy in all the wrong places.

I have found this psalm so inspiring at a time when my future is uncertain. It helps me to believe, to trust and it lays life out very simply for me. It's like a boy scouts guide to a 'good life', to a life that wants to be consumed by God.

Life with God is meant to be simple. Fearing God, that's wisdom. Being His friend, that's pure bliss.

Rebecca St. James is a Grammy Award winning Christian singer whose album sales are in the millions. She is also a spokesperson for the True Love Waits movement which advocates sexual abstinence until marriage.

Rebecca St James

2 Corinthians 3 v 18

> 18 But we all, with open face beholding as in a glass the glory of the Lord, are changed into the same image from glory to glory, even as by the Spirit of the Lord.
>
> 2 Corinthians 3 v 18

One of my good friends has a daughter who is two. I love to rollerblade by the beach where I live while pushing this little girl in her pram! She squeals with joy and lifts up her head and hands, expressing the freedom she feels. Little Ava's face is a visual representation of the open, unveiled countenance that we can have as children of God.

If the eyes are the window to the soul, then people have the ability to look into our hearts every day; at the grocery store, at work, on the street, and at home. Pain, tragedy, and disappointment can veil and shadow our eyes. It can darken them and hide the love and hope we can offer to others, through them. By looking to God each day, we can be changed by encountering His glory. Our faces can begin to reflect His image and our eyes can be opened, lightened.

This verse reminds me to draw close to God each day; in Christian community, in giving, in reading the Bible, in prayer, in worship and in thankfulness. The joy of encountering Him and His love for me, will unveil my face and I will become more like Him. And more like a little girl in a pram by the beach, propelled by someone who loves her.

GP Taylor is the New York Times' best-selling author of the 'Shadowmancer' books.

G P Taylor

> 35 Jesus wept.
>
> John 11 v 35

Perhaps not the longest of quotes from the Bible, but for me the most poignant.

In my search for faith I looked at many beliefs before becoming a Christian. I have dabbled in paganism and the occult and examined Buddhism and the paranormal. In all of my searching I never found a deity that had compassion – until I found Jesus.

The Gospel of John is a fine piece of writing about the life of Jesus. It shows Him as the Son of God and to have Him weep is the most beautiful and touching thing that I know. It was what attracted me to Christianity – God was compassionate to the point where He would not only weep for me but also be prepared to die for me. My life has been such that I have and do get things wrong all the time. I am a fallen man in a frail world, and I am so grateful to have found a Saviour who is prepared to weep over the world.

In many ways I have faced hardships throughout my life and it has been the greatest strength to know that I am loved by God and so important to Him. God is not a man in the sky or a deity waiting to smite the world, but to me is a compassionate loving creator who was prepared to give the life of someone He loved so I could live and have a relationship with Him. This is truly amazing stuff. God weeps over a broken world - over lives lost and selfish wars. God weeps over our greed and neglect, religious fundamentalism and killing in His name.

Jesus wept tender tears for the loss of His friend, but those tears were turned to joy when He overcame death once and for all. Even in the darkest moments those two words give me hope that a loving God will give me rest and eternal peace. All I have to do to inherit this is believe that Jesus is the Son of God and to confess that in a world that doesn't want to hear. A world that Jesus weeps for today.

The face of BBC 1's Saturday lunchtime Football Focus, Dan Walker, has covered everything from Six Nations rugby to the Grand National. Dan is also a regular on Match of the Day.

5 Let this mind be in you, which was also in Christ Jesus:
6 Who, being in the form of God, thought it not robbery to be equal with God:
7 But made himself of no reputation, and took upon him the form of a servant, and was made in the likeness of men:
8 And being found in fashion as a man, he humbled himself, and became obedient unto death, even the death of the cross.

Philippians 2 v 5-8

Dan Walker

Philippians 2 v 5-8

When Augustine of Hippo was asked for three words to sum up Jesus Christ, the story goes that he responded with … "Humility, humility, humility." I think he was right and that's what these verses are all about.

Jesus is to be our example in all parts of life but I feel there are few areas we fall so far short of His standards. Today greatness is measured by how much we have – money, cars, friends – but here we have Christ measured by how much He was ready to give up – for us.

I find these verses amazing because they are talking about the truth that the almighty God became a man. The kings of kings was born in Bethlehem and lived on this earth in poverty. I live in a 3-bed-terrace but all that He had was borrowed. The stable – not His, a place to lay His head – not His, a boat to preach from, a donkey to ride into Jerusalem, a room to remember the Passover in… none of it was His because He 'made himself of no reputation'. He knew that life would be hard and short of what we consider pleasure but He lived a life marked by humility and – even more mind blowing – He died in the same way.

These verses always remind me that Jesus was as obedient as He was humble. He was born in obedience to His Father's will, lived in perfect obedience to it, and died an obedient servant. I find obedience difficult when nothing's at stake – Christ's obedience was perfect when everything was at stake and all because He loved the unlovable. He came to set guilty sinners free.

CS Lewis said that 'pride was the mother hen under which all other sins are hatched'. A fraction of Christ's humility would transform our lives. When I think about the lengths He went to that I might have life – I ask myself this question: do I see a self-sacrificing life, marked by obedience to God's word, as the best life I can lead? These verses always make me stop and think.

Ann Widdecombe was one of the most popular stars on the BBC's Strictly Come Dancing show. A leading pro-life campaigner, she stepped down from the House of Commons at the 2010 General Election after 23 years.

3 Simon Peter saith unto them, I go a fishing. They say unto him, We also go with thee. They went forth, and entered into a ship immediately; and that night they caught nothing.

4 But when the morning was now come, Jesus stood on the shore: but the disciples knew not that it was Jesus.

5 Then Jesus saith unto them, Children, have ye any meat? They answered him, No.

6 And he said unto them, Cast the net on the right side of the ship, and ye shall find. They cast therefore, and now they were not able to draw it for the multitude of fishes.

7 Therefore that disciple whom Jesus loved saith unto Peter, It is the Lord. Now when Simon Peter heard that it was the Lord, he girt *his* fisher's coat *unto him*, (for he was naked,) and did cast himself into the sea.

8 And the other disciples came in a little ship; (for they were not far from land, but as it were two hundred cubits,) dragging the net with fishes.

9 As soon then as they were come to land, they saw a fire of coals there, and fish laid thereon, and bread.

10 Jesus saith unto them, Bring of the fish which ye have now caught.

11 Simon Peter went up, and drew the net to land full of great fishes, an hundred and fifty and three: and for all there were so many, yet was not the net broken.

12 Jesus saith unto them, Come *and* dine. And none of the disciples durst ask him, Who art thou? knowing that it was the Lord.

John 21 v 3-12

Ann Widdecombe

John 21 v 3-12

I've always warmed to Peter. He represents all that's best and worst in a follower of Jesus. Peter is passionate, headstrong and not very politically correct. Yet, he is also loyal, humble and willing to learn and improve.

When John tells Peter that Jesus is standing on the shore, he jumps into the water to swim across. Peter just wants to be with his Lord again. That's what you call passion. Remember, Peter was the apostle who declared Jesus to be the Messiah. He was the leader of this little band of men who gave up everything to follow the Lord. He was also the apostle who denied his Lord three times.

Like Peter many of us today can blow hot and cold in our faith. There are Christians who risk their livelihood or their very lives by declaring their love of Jesus. We need to remember and pray for those who suffer imprisonment and death just for being Christians. Thank God, most of us do not face such trials; yet, we can meet ridicule or disdain in the workplace, in our families and now from the militant atheists who are very vociferous in our society. At times, we may feel, like Peter, it would be prudent to deny our Lord. That would give us an easier life, yet a very unfulfilled one. We are always drawn back to Him who gladly welcomes us.

And how does the Lord show His love? This passage comes after He has been through the Crucifixion, been ridiculed, suffered excruciating pain and even rejection by the apostles, like Peter, who had previously declared their love for Him. What does Jesus now do? He cooks breakfast. Love in the small things, love in the big things.

The 104th Archbishop of Canterbury, Rowan Williams was the first Welshman to hold the title when he was apointed on 27 February 2003. Dr Williams is acknowledged internationally as an outstanding theological writer, scholar and teacher.

Archbishop of Canterbury
Rowan Williams

2 Corinthians 3 v 18

> 18 But we all, with open face beholding as in a glass the glory of the Lord, are changed into the same image from glory to glory, *even* as by the Spirit of the Lord.
>
> 2 Corinthians 3 v 18

We become what we gaze at: that seems to be the message of this verse. It is so condensed in meaning that it would take a long time to spell it out, but it seems to be saying that, when our true humanity is revealed in Christ, then, when we look into the mirror, when we try to see ourselves truthfully, we are overtaken by the reflection of the radiance that has been given to us, even as we struggle with all the ways we have failed. And God continues to strip away the veils, so that more and more of His beauty is uncovered. This is the Spirit's work as the Spirit brings Christ more and more to life in us.

The KJV is written to be read aloud and heard. That is why it still retains such a resonance for so many people. Words are given their full weight, and the pattern of words, just as in the original Greek and (even more) Hebrew, is allowed its proper 'music'. So, in a culture where we are not used to paying such attention to the music of our words, and where we don't often write with a view to being heard, the KJV has a special significance and value. It puts us in touch with something of the experience of the original world of the Bible, and that must be a particularly important contribution to our receiving of God's gift in Scripture.

Bible Society
Stonehill Green
Westlea
Swindon
SN5 7DG

biblesociety.org.uk

Tel: 01793 418222

Charity Reg. No 232759
Patron: Her Majesty the Queen

The following photographs are by courtesy of Adam Greene –
Jeff Lucas
Peter Owen-Jones
Ann Widdicombe
Dr Rowan Williams